There Shines Forth Christ

verse, by Dom Julian Stead

with an introduction by Sheldon Vanauken,
author of A Severe Mercy

ST. BEDE'S PUBLICATIONS
STILL RIVER, MASSACHUSETTS

Nihil Obstat:

Dom Kevin Seasoltz, O.S.B.
Censor Librorum

Imprimatur:

Rt. Rev. Victor Farwell, O.S.B.
Abbot President
English Benedictine Congregation

The Nihil obstat and Imprimatur are official declarations that
the manuscript is free of doctrinal or moral error.

LIBRARY OF CONGRESS CATALOGING IN PUBLICATION DATA

Stead, Julian.
    There shines forth Christ verse.

    Includes index.
    1. Christian poetry, American. I. Title.
PS3569.T3368T5   1983   811'.54   83-3382
ISBN 0-932506-29-1

CONTENTS

Part IV—Rome

Part V—Rhode Island

Part VI—Afterthoughts

to
the memory of
W.F.S.

ACKNOWLEDGEMENTS

"The Catch," "Release," "Lamb of God," and "October Hunting" reprinted with permission from *Commonweal.* "Red River" reprinted with permission from *Living City.* "Wells Cathedral" copyright © 1978; "Faith" copyright © 1979; "Matthew," "The High Lands," "And the Word Was God," "Oblation," Copyright © 1980; "Out There," "Scottish Rain" (published as "Rain in Scotland"), Copyright © 1981; "Christ," "Creaturehood," "Grievously Lamenting," "The Rejected Land," copyright © 1982. Reprinted with permission from the *New Oxford Review* (6013 Lawton Avenue, Oakland, CA 94618). "Thanks Be to God," "Ah Studio!" "Cry to the Night," and "Fall Evening" from *A Severe Mercy* by Sheldon Vanauken. Copyright © 1977, 1980, by Sheldon Vanauken. Reprinted with permission of Harper & Row, Publishers, Inc. (published in England by Hodder & Stoughton).

Cover photo by Salvatore Mancini.

INTRODUCTION

Never shall I, never could I, write an introduction more
willingly and joyously than this one to the poems of my dear
friend, Dom Julian of the Order of St Benedict. The willing-
ness of course stems from the friendship, but the joy springs
from long-standing belief that his poetry is, quite simply, the
finest Christian poetry in English of our times.

Thirty years ago amidst the 'dreaming spires' of Oxford a
friend brought round to the Studio a slender young man
wearing a clerical 'dog collar,' introducing him as Brother
Julian of St Benet's Hall. The Studio, named by some forgotten
predecessor, was a tiny mews flat with a skylight where my
wife Davy (Jean) and I lived. Its great merit was being located
on a cobbled and gaslit lane in the heart of Oxford, and its
outer door knocker was rarely silent for long. We liked Julian
at once—a quiet manner and a smile that lighted up his face.
He had only recently come to Oxford from his studies in Rome;
and we were glad to know him, not in spite of but because he
bore the mark of Christ's service, for we, not long before, had
put away our agnosticism for that same Lord, there in Oxford;
and the world had become bright. There by the Studio fireside
the walls echoed with talk about the Faith, night after night
talk and laughter and frequent joy; and Julian with his
humour and his love of the living Christ fitted into the Studio
scene as though we had been waiting for him to turn up.

Although Davy and I were C of E, we held to the brotherhood
of believers, and I, at least, was drawn by Holy Mother Church.
Moreover, we shared with Julian a deep love of England and of
the American South. We, Davy and I, had come to Oxford from
Virginia; and Julian, although born in England, had done
much of his growing up in Maryland, his family rooted in the

wide-watered Eastern Shore. And we ourselves had sailed the tidal rivers and coasts of the Eastern Shore in our schooner *Grey Goose*. Even more important than origins, I discovered almost at once that Julian, too was a poet—next to Christ Himself, the deepest possible link, especially with both of us writing our poems for the glory of God. "Julian's poetry," I wrote in my book about Oxford days and later, *A Severe Mercy*, "Julian's poetry was pure prayer, deep and holy."

One night at the Studio, when several of us were gathered together in His name, the talk turned to whom among the New Testament folk each of us felt the closest to, apart from Our Lord. Somebody, possibly I, said he felt closest to the often-blundering St Peter. Mary Magdalene and St John were mentioned. Davy, rather to my surprise, said she felt closest to St Paul. Julian was silent. "Well, Julian?" I said. In a low voice he said, "The Good Thief...crucified with Him." Then *we* were silent in a sort of holy astonishment, wishing perhaps that we had had the humility to think of that. It was the measure of the man.

On an April morning Davy and I went to Julian's priesting at nearby Blackfriars, thinking of certain poems of his leading up to this longed-for moment, particularly the poem in which he spoke of "walking in the garden...Pawing with the foot of my philosophy the dust of the path...In the swallowswooping time of the evening" whilst he sought "uncaring unknowingness and unreasoned trust" (page 4). And the ordination poem itself in which he offered to Christ his all: "Tormented thought and worn-out shoes, / Take all and dwell therein" (page 24).

Remembering our friendship in those long-gone days, I find images crowding round: the two of us walking along the Isis by the college barges, going to a lecture together at Blackfriars and talking about it afterwards, a walk to Perch with skylarks singing, a long talk by the fire one night about the Blessed Virgin that led me to write a sonnet about her dedicated lovingly to Julian, a long walk round Dorchester in Oxfordshire where Julian's childhood parish church was—a walk that ended with brown ale in the local pub. And I remember an atheist girl speaking of meeting him on the street: "His face

xiv

was like a light…almost I could believe." But, above all, I remember talking in the late night hours, talking gently by the fire of our Christ, while the slow rain fell on the skylight and the bells of Oxford rang out the hours. Then with a prayer and a "Go under the Mercy" from Davy or me, he would be off to nearby St Benet's (see "Pusey Lane," page 84).

It was a magical time for all of us, but our golden Oxford afternoon could not go on for ever. Julian went down first, back to his Rhode Island monastery, whence he sent us a poem of longing for Oxford ("Fall Evening," page 84). Then we, too, must say goodbye to the city of our souls, sailing in winter for Virginia. But the poem that, more than any other by either of us, sums up (and summons up) our friendship then and its meaning was to be written decades later, after Davy had been taken to her Lord and I was writing my book about it, sending each chapter to Julian as it was written. Reading the Oxford chapters, he was moved to write "Ah Studio!" that perfectly catches it all (page 86).

At the Virginian college where I taught, a student group gathered round Davy and me to hear of Christ. There, too, we had a fireside, and Julian, though he was far away, was also there. Almost every evening when we met, the students would ask me to read some poems, and I would finish always with some of Julian's.

There would be lamplight on my poembook and in the room firelight—the warm glow of a coal fire—and the students on the floor. I would read, not only many of those I've mentioned but "Oblation" (page 8), which made them smile, or "The High Lands" (page 74), which awed them. "Wells Cathedral" (page 75) was a favourite and "After a Walk" (page 14), and I would finish with "Thanks Be to God" (page 3), which came to mean so much to Davy. There would be pauses after each poem, and we would stare silently into the fire. Then a silent prayer, with only each one's half-whispered "Amen," and the students would go away into the night, sped by our "Go under the Mercy." Julian was as much a part of those evenings as he'd have been in person.

Although the Christian group would go on afterwards, the loving warmth of Davy's presence was to be removed by death

in a few short years. She was not a poet: her art was painting—
and perhaps loving. But not long before her death, she did
write a poem whence the title of this book is taken. I cannot
close more fittingly than by giving her poem from *A Severe
Mercy*.

Dear dying Julian
Gracious and just
Dying to self
And hid deep in Christ

Still thou dost live
In pain and thirst
And bit by bit
Consume to dust

Thy soul's dark night
Works life in us
To our dim vision
There shines forth Christ

Ah! but how fair
Thy bare faith is
Refuge for us
Who still do not trust

—Sheldon Vanauken

*On August 15, 1981 Sheldon Vanauken was received into the
Catholic Church by Dom Julian Stead.*

Thanks Be To God

THANKS BE TO GOD

If everything is lost, thanks be to God
If I must see it go, watch it go,
Watch it fade away, die
Thanks be to God that He is all I have
And if I have Him not, I have nothing at all
Nothing at all, only a farewell to the wind
Farewell to the grey sky
Goodbye, God be with you, evening October sky.
If all is lost, thanks be to God,
For He is He, and I am only I.

UNREASONED TRUST

O God give me wisdom
Me walking in the garden in the shadows of the setting sun
Pawing with the foot of my philosophy the dust of the path
Renouncing all my knowledge confessing
my pure unknowingness
In the swallowswooping time of the evening breathing
When earth and all of me takes a last flight and returns
   to the nest
Of uncaring unknowingness and unreasoned trust
Of uncaring unknowingness and unreasoned trust
Of the grave of the choir stall and the grave of the bedroom
Of the wood of the choir stall and the wood of the cell door
Where the mystery shines in its utter blackness
To which we were born God You and I were born

AND THE WORD WAS GOD

(God the Father speaks)

All alone, in my completeness,
In the single instant of the dawning noontime
And sunset glory of my only day
My mind has looked into the heaven
Of sunlit moonlight, its own beauty—
In tears it spoke one Word
One sound which sings a symphony
Where all tone and melody were born.

Good God! it cries, for it is I.

Among the stars beyond all number,
The light that's one,
From star to star we dance together,
Eyes in eyes,
From thought to thought, and all in one,
We move together.
This is the blessedness of our dancing song.
This is the dance that you have heard of,
in the center.

Now in our speed we see, from eye to eye,
And hear each other's voice, our self,
In this our love-song,
Feel the music of our throbbing dance of unison
At once we spot that which has happened,
What we wanted,
Love is born from our song,

5

But in the song
Glistens in the tears like a galaxy
Our eyes and voice are breathing
Expiring, exhaling
Spirit, like the wind of dawn, noon, and evening,
From end to end of us, of me,
Our comfort, and our joy. So be our joy.

THE AEON

The aeon and its kingdom,
ruled beyond cloud or air,
stabs the heart with longing,
the selfish belly with fear.

The King stands
thousands of miles high

robed in the sanctity
of saints who cry,
"You made us what we are,
pale blue—peaceful hue—
deep red, through blood shed
and work done on coasts, far
from coddling home and woods nigh
our fleshly hearts."

Green with the sap of perpetual spring
Christ's saints play their parts
of clothing him
in glory, and golden darts
fly round him from their eyes of prayer;
and orange Seraphim
praise him for the care
with which they preached his name.
Indigo blue the oceans of the wise
with wild power drowning the tame
ignorance of the dry
who are all-knowing in their own eyes.
Violet stamps the presses, from which fly
the messages which circulate through heart and mind
to all the glorious clothing of the King;
pure white the strands of unity which bind
each soul to harmony and make God's city sing.

OBLATION

A sacrifice and oblation we offer to the Father
Our own lives brought down like a pheasant in late autumn
Broken blind warm and dead
May what is left of us be acceptable to Thee
We bring what we are, not what we would be
To us it looks like Comedy
Though pride would have it Tragedy.

The audience are bored and have all walked away
And I am left alone, better leave the stage,
It is only an ice floe slowly melting.
Soon I shall be alone and very wet
And very cold, in the lower Arctic
Up to my neck, that will be the end.

And there will be glory to the Father
And to the Son and to the Holy Ghost
As it was in the beginning
Is now
And ever shall be
Amen.
But how *this* shall be His glory
I cannot ask or tell.

THE REJECTED LAND

It is hot and wraps you round
It is for you alone
To raise your sun in the empty sky
And let it beam on the grey lake waters
Till they sparkle
Till they're blue
Circled by the green
And wild rose.
None but your sun will ever see
This rolling land
Surrounded by forbidding alps
Inviolate in their privacy
Only your horse shall tread these paths
Thread these forest-shaded shadows
It's your own land
And will stand
No other prince but you.
But you
Cast off its proffered crown.
Unruled unvisited and closed
Its flowers fade, its trees have drowned
Bleak in fog and rain
And noontime darkness
Nothing grows
No fisher's feet wade the streams
No steeds will gallop down the valley roads
For your sun withdrew its beams and rose
On some other valley, strange mountains,
In some foreign world.

CREATUREHOOD

I am nothing, not a snowflake
Melting in the air,
Not a current of wind that could move
A tree, a branch, a leaf,—a hair
Upon the forehead of a skiing girl.
Existence is not me. How do I dare
Complain that I am nothing, have no life,
As if the world began in me, or here
History should find its guide?
I am but a path rubbed out in time,
I'm not its end, nor either side,
Nor the crossroad where
It meets no time. I'll hide
In my own hole of nothingness
Under the blanket of prayer, year after year.

GRIEVOUSLY LAMENTING

Grievously lamenting
I seek You in the dark.
You come and leave.
Your departure is dementing
For You're always there,
But dogs bark
And drive You away for other thoughts,
Or bells ring, to mark
Duties that distract and grieve.
Rather would the soul be tenting
In Your desert here
Round sand and rock, moonstone and quartz,
As the fire cools. I breathe
The gentle wind, repenting
All the past;
And fire turns to light
Turns off the dark desire and fear
And I forget the last
              Good night.

HACELDAMA*

In the Rockies there's a field of blood,
Haceldama—
Where the horses canter, and the thud
(It's hell's drummer)
Of laughing hooves, all snorting in the dust's
Vast acreage,
Beats a blood-red soul and thrusts
To canyon edge
His faithless feet, there to drop forever,
For betrayal's kiss, of flesh for flesh,
Like so many
Who loved Christ in the creche
But sent his rejected face
To Pilate, to bury.

*"Field of Blood" Aramaic (Acts 1:19)

SEA MOON

The moon is the landlord of the night
His face impassive and his movement unharried, unhurried
He watches men die and marry and be born
He looks down through lowered eyelids
And watches what he does not see
How can he hear the mouth gasping in the ocean?
Lift up your voice and cry
He cannot hear
Your voice cannot fill the sea and sky
Go down
The way down is the way upward
Darkness down, never to see
The unfeeling starlight
But the sweet salt dark and the brightness
Of the deep height.

SO COLD

So cold, September morning.
Cold wraps itself around the bones
At day and winter's dawning.
The day will not be long; like stones
However, laid around me
The winter nights are heaped to stay
And be my grave, surround me
With hate I cannot drive away
       And so I'm buried and alone
       Until Your love moves back the stone.

AFTER A WALK

Why does the rain lie like grief in my hair
Why does the drizzle symbolize despair
Why has the yearly rainfall taught my heart
To hope no more in this hour of air
To live apart
From this cloud-filled earth
To walk where birth
Nor death mean ought but
Christ and living there.

GRIEF

O grief, you flow between
Me and my Lord unseen
On your other bank;

And I must thank
The mist of diffidence and doubt
And puzzlement, the sun will not come out.

O reach between, great heart,
Push the drops of mist apart
And let me see,

Look in His eyes, the sunlight round His hair,
One glimpse of all men's love, God's heir.

DARK

Has there been a break in it
The soundless cry?
Has there been any relenting to the cry, cry,
Cry from the hollow dark?
Cry to the height of invisible light.
Light which cannot penetrate
Unless on the waves of the comprehending cry.
Do not ask what to cry,
The hollow resounds best with silence
And the horror-struck eye
Sees best in the stillness of dark.
Only one Voice can fill
And thrill
This hollow void.

DARK HOUR

When the long tired day has sighed and reclined to sleep
Then (dark hour) under the canopy of the trees
Hearken to that heart beating
Feel the blood pulsing
Through the earth it has redeemed
Recapitulating it all in Him

THE MAP OF LIFE

Take your old, thumbed map of life
And with the wet matches of your faith, read the way.
Through the walls, o'er the paths, some day
To high road you may come
And meet the pilgrim crowd of loving men
Walking towards the rising of the Sun.

STRAIGHT ON

Straight on to windward where winter glooms
Straight on straight through
Steer on, His faith is true
Who on the quayside waits and fumes
In incense prayers
Who through you steers
Me into harbor blue and clear
Into harbor over there
Beyond the winter and the storm
Beyond this awful day of fear.

16

OUR HEARTH

The hearth we sit around is prayer,
At desk and choir-stall: there
The warmth of love bounds forth
In stationary fire;
Within the house of faith the north
And night of self retire
Shut out the door, and hot desire
Lights up the air,
Runs through the hair,
As morning sunrise brightly tints the spire.

HERMIT'S SONG

Give me a wild moor
I will search it up and down
And there I shall find
Thee,
There on the heathered moor
Free as the thistledown
Alone, I will only mind
Thee.

FAITH
(Mark 8:27-33)

Dare to go with you, be seen with you,
Listen in silence while you speak and touch and heal,
Or while you're spat on, questioned, nailed and left to die—
Do people call you prophet now?
No, "myth". Make me believe that you are real:
Messiah, priest and king,
Creator, born to suffer and to die
Alone, despised, to rise
Living by the standard rule of God,
In every man and place,
Poor and young, rich and old,
Judged not nor condemned but loved
With worship, in each who's rich in faith
With faith to give, and faith to strengthen him,
From him whose gift it is.

O JESUS, MY ONCE LOVE

O Jesus, my once love for thee was fire
Unfeigned, aglow, and melting out my sins:
Like perspiration, tears throbbed in desire
From every pore. Thus life in Spring begins.
The life of faith and in thy Father trust
Once budded forth in seldom-broken thought,
Intense sustained heartbreak. In this life must
The growing Spring, O Lord, give way to naught,
The barren emptiness of arid cold?
What was both source and goal of warmth now bores
My chill embittered brain, and I am old
No more a child whose trusting smile adores.
   Consign these bones beneath thy Cross's ground
   And let me fly to Light and ever circle round.

WHERE WILL I FALL?

Never mind, for as I fall from cloud to cloud
Out of the universe
Though you nor either I see the way
It is there always
So do not look to see me go, to shout beware,
To gesticulate, to call,
Nor speculate, O where, O where will he fall?
Where we live, your level path and my downward one
Lead to the same.
Do not fear. In the end I will not fall
But alight on my toe
Quietly, to greet my Father's hand.

STORM

I thank thee because
I have known thee
On stormy nights,
Seeing lightning over fields, between
Clouds whose silver eyes
Glistened in rain pools.

I found the way, around
The second tree
Then up and up the hill,
Either the storm or
The rising moon has shown
Clear enough the path
To thy will.

HOPE

Shall I depart the smoothly pavéd way
Of faith and its conviction, joy, and hope?
Better perhaps admitting to the day
I have no faith at all, no stay, no scope
On which to found my hope of here, hereafter,—
Naught but faithlessness, damnation, and despair,
Till the laughter
Hell is full of sucks me in its throat
There to gloat
On him who had no hope...
No, You alone,
Great Nazarene, lover of men's souls
Will garland me with hope,
And gird me round with fortitude
To face the role
Of witness to the Pope
And preacher of the faith with certitude.

NOT MY WILL

Keep me sadly
on my root
let me give a scent
distinct and soft
or bright.

Growing badly
proud to boot
whatever flower you meant
was swept aloft
from sight.

Love me madly
always shoot
dangers round my tent
or fence, which gnaw
and bite.

PRAYER FOR ORDINATION

Come to my lips blood of chalice,
Come from the great west window. Come!
For gold I offer discouragement, for incense prayer,
For myrrh temptations in a tomb of sin.
The journey, Christ, has brought me here
White-robed and clean-washed within,
Give me your chalice, Lord, and I will give
Tormented thought and worn-out shoes,
Take all and dwell there in.

TRUE VINE

True Vine
All thy roots about me twine,
Suck my blood to make it Thine,
One sap, thy blood and mine:
My love
Above
The years
Of tears.
To find eternal sky
Draw me from time on high,
Through root and stalk, until the hour
When mud from me becomes thy flower.

24

COMMUNION

Who am I
That I should stand
And reach down
To your open mouth
And hand you Him
Whom you meet
With a young kiss
Like its first morning
A rose will meet
The divine dew
Its petals parted
In love to their life
Who am I
That I should see
This with Him
Your intimacy—
On these moments
Why trespass I
To glance with God
Upon the love
Meant for Him?

CHRIST

All of a sudden, come to me.
Make me forget. When we can see
The most beautiful face
So radiant with grace
Clothed with foliage of glory,
No longer will we be sorry,
Living in pain and fearing war.
Peace will come in through the door
Because we are One, now
That prayer has taught us how
We live for You alone
In sickness and health, gone
The painless years of youth
Come the hours of ruth
And daily crucifixion,
Knowing You are no fiction,
And after burial will come Your glory.
The morning after a tornado's fury
Could bring no peace nor redder dawn
In deeper contrast to what had gone
Before, than You when You arrive
With friendship, joy which must survive
For it's the glow of no illusion,
In stead the everlasting, warm diffusion
Of bright reality, no tube-fed screen

But incorruption that has been
Glorified in (mystery) undying, risen flesh.
Give it to me, to embrace and eat it fresh
And let it coinhere with mine
Like alcohol within the wine,
Until no later than forever—
Conscious, thinking, loving, never
Tired, distracted, bored or called away.
Come now, at midnight, silent splendid Day.

NEW YORK DESTROYED

Where once the girls
Had not an eyelash out of place
The sand swirls
Upon a hill where seagulls croak or rest
O joy that You have taught us
What is joy, and where,
And have destroyed
Our loneliness, where we were crowded,
And all the grief
That we had gloated in,
And made the chief
Of all our gaudy idols.

A STAR

Looking through the screen I see a star,
But it was not that far.
I thought it was light years away,
But it was not a day,
Only an hour.
He came for me.
"Enough," he said, "you've had enough.
You've had to wait too long.
Now that you know you're not the stuff
This world is made of, you belong
Where you can flower,
And always see
Your star, not through a screen
But round about you like a shower
Bursting from within,
Till you are rain still standing in the tower
Of ivory to stay
A rainbow forever in my ray
Image of my glory and my power."

THESE ARE THE DAYS OF NIGHT

These are the days of night,
A time to grope, to touch, and find,
To love, not yet to see.
This is the day to be
Afire with such a hope as wined
The thief upon thy right.

We have not much but sparks
Put out from the eternal fire,
Bearing more love than light,
Understanding recondite
Inciting fevers of desire
And branding slavery's marks.

Thy slave soon finds he's free
With all we know put out,
Diplomas burned in holy fire;
When candles shall grow dark,
Thy face shall say, "Now hark,
Here is some work to never tire,
Know now, you cannot doubt."

In silence I take flight
Leaving all sight and sound behind
Leaving all hope to thee
No other goal or guide shall be
But suddenly worlds are intertwined
Dark ignorance made bright.

THE LUMP

Because I hate
to be
because I do not love
Thee
Thou only art beautiful
forever
young and old will fall
for Thee
as long as men and women
will ever

Because it is not late
to beg
kneeling by the corridor
on bended leg
grant me to be dutiful
in prayer
until I'm old enough
to swear
that it was good and better
to believe
and live
to have been forgiven

You looked for me
but I was out to eat
or up in bed
You sought me
but I was lost
and lost my head

I flirted with a camera and a joke
to buy some powdered friend
a smile built of dust
You offered me a yearlong feast
if I'd no longer turn my back
to gorge on hair and leather
we'd be together
as long as no old yearning lust
or paradise to south or east
should send
treacherous mind through heart crack.

OUR FATHER

If it is true, then you must look
To no one but to Him
Whom you shall never see
Until from all your friends and world
And from this painful body you are free.
He is so close, the cause of mind
And yet we cannot know
The Who and What and how,
Or ever find
A way to touch, to show
With trembling hand
The reverence and the passion of the love that now
Would burn if we could find a way
Or understand
There is no way, but only say
Our Father—
Replies the omnipresent Silence:
My child, believe
And on your credence
Cease to grieve.

THY NAME

I don't know why the mind reaches out
to thy Name,
But whether in the seething sea
that gnashes white teeth above
with deep savagery,
Or whether in the muddy flood waters
sucking at the sills of poor men's houses,
Always the heart must seek its rest in thee,
pure light on a muddy sea.

EVERY TREE

The world is always autumn.
Falling leaves
Whose names are children
Wives and parents
Honors praise
And holidays.
And every tree grows naked and alone, again,
As it was when but a seed
Before it saw the sky:
Every tree grows blind again
Unless the fire
Should lift it up
Where every leaf and blossom did aspire.

LINES

Lines on a lady's face
are no disgrace.
Railroad lines
are dead in shock.
Lines on a page
are a nice invitation.
Lines in perspective
can beckon and mock:
draw me right,
and explore what I point to,
what's your fright?
Jump, I await you.
Afraid of getting hit
head on,
or from the side?
All alone,
down along the line
to nowhere,
must wait something,
dark, or light.

NOW

Clear memory of all,
bring grace
unimaginable,
light like a trumpet
from many miles away,
birdsong,
one cardinal by the branch,
challenging the American hell to imitate
—impossibility—
the sweet glory
of his love.

Sun on a running stream,
a beam
of song into the spring leaves;
sound of a girl's steps
on the fall twigs;
all seasons blend in silence
where a man alone
forgets
and finds the future now.

A PRAYER FOR CHRISTMAS NIGHT

Night of nights wild in the north-west wind
Bitter cold as a foreboding song
Telling of children's death, cruel murder,
Flight in the desert, escaping to the cold.
—Much later to the mountains, the loneliness of prayer,
Alone in the mountain places God's own prayer
Rising higher and higher gathering disciples there,
To lose them all in the hour of the ghastly sin.
O God, let me die with thee, let me not run away
I who was born again in thy naked cold
On this new Christmas Day.

YOU ARE ALL BEAUTIFUL*

Only you are beautiful, the winter sky
Is your blue head-and-shoulder veil
The freshly fallen snow your dress
Let me build an igloo there, and hide
From the bitterness of winter's wail
Like an eskimo babe between your breasts
Wrap me round with your bright blue veil
And caress
What you alone can guide.

*Tota Pulchra Es, Maria—Latin antiphon

36

THUNDERCLOUDS

More expansive than a thundercloud
And blacker than despair
Voices from creation sing aloud
Crows, and ocean winds and waves, break the morning air.
Broods on chilly rock the ghost of war,
A poet placed him there
Brewing hatred colder to the core,
Till the bloodied clouds of evening sank before the stars
Of innocence, when the moon,
New moon, and stars made light appear;
Mother of peace, lady of the night,
Through death this world has passed
Into your beams, no fright
Could make it shiver when it cast
Its faith onto your sight.

WHAT DID SHE WEAR?

What did she wear
When she went out to meet her son?
(His will be done)
How did she dress
To see him on this stroll
Out the gate and out the wall
With what did she prepare?
What kind of shoes? Any?
Her robe and veil
Were they new? What color, bright, dark, or pale?
Clean? As a bright penny?
Did she ask advice—
"Dear, would this be nice
When one does not know what will happen?
Being a widow, and having just one son
What does one put on, after what they've done?"
Had you any choice, another wrapping?
"No." Neither have I,
For it is too late
(His will be done).

GOOD FRIDAY

All the eleven now are weeping,
All God's Israel is sad.
The sword to Mary's heart is creeping.
Thieves are cursing. Ghosts awaken.
Down in the city tell the news is bad:
Jesus Christ has been forsaken
To His pains no more can add.

All the sorrows of all sinners
Were twisted round His head.
All His blood, to try and win us
To His love for us, He's shed.
Down on the stony ground His mother stayed
While the Jews prepared their dinners
and Satan thought that God was dead.

RED RIVER

A river rose
And flooded in my window

A river red

It washed my chairs and books away
And soaked my bed

I can no longer sit and read
I can no longer sleep
Or lay down my head
Except the damp reminder flows
Of where that red river rose
Under thorns and scourge, the day
That some one bled.

MOCKERY

Did that back bleed? Was it not sticky and warm
to the touch of the lechers' lash?

Stones beneath his trembling feet
kneel, methodical scourges beat,
weave, o scourge, your kiss of hate,
weep, temple, tears of stone;
break, veil, with every heart,
but beat, lash our death away,
suffer, sufferer, stay, stay,
shame us till we come your way
which first we laid for you,
where friends betray;
stay, stay till the lance shall fix us too.

What do your thorns say?
You cannot think except of us all day,
and we are almost to the brain.
Shall we twist those thorns again?
Shall we wear your skullbone thin?
Or shall we beg you, give that crown to me
and may it twist our reeling brain,
until we see
who bought the crown of misery,
and take with you that victory
under the load of shame,
and add your royal title to our name.

ENCLOSURE

Jesus went out, and his disciples, into the towns of Caesarea Philippi: and by the way he asked..., Whom do men say that I am?   Mark 8:27-30

Jesus in seclusion
Will forgive
A man who wants to live
In prayer without intrusion.
Disciples may be with Him
But not to interfere
With the work of prayer
Where flesh and spirit swim.

He wonders what we think of Him.
Do You care
In my sight to bare
How holy and how beautiful, to my sight so dim,
Is Your true nature?
I'll not hate Your
Heart, Your words, nor will;
While You drive my nails,
For You are the Messiah,
You really will not kill
Except the bent desire.

JUDAS

Even at night
He knew the way
But only to betray.

By the light
Of the full moon
He found You very soon.

For the last time
Then he kissed You
But he had badly missed You.

With one last crime
He left the altar
For he preferred a halter.

ZEBEDEE SPEAKS

My favorite son was James
How he cast his net around!
I cannot tilt my boat
But that I think of James
So quiet and so strong
Reluctantly I saw him go
With grief I heard that Herod
—I cannot say it, I can only say
The smile has left my throat
I cannot tilt my boat
But that I think of James.

MATTHEW

Jesus saw a man doing a disgraceful job
And told him, "Follow me."
Never again did Matthew work for the Roman.
That did not, though, make him popular with the mob.

What would his tomorrow be
He never knew, for he was Jesus' yeoman.
Jesus would decide. That he did believe and trust.
And took Him home to eat.

That was a lesson of life, little he knew it,
Only it seemed to show gratitude, which show he must
And bring his friends to meet
Their Saviour with His mercy, letting them view it.

44

OUT THERE

(for St Peter)

They're crucifying my Rabbi
out there
and I'm scared
this was my third year
with him
I know not what I'll do
I believed he had the answers
to our problems and our hopes
he could do everything
not just teach
walk on the sea
cure the sick and the mad
bring back the dead
you smile? I've seen him
more often than I could count
but he cannot save himself.

I wonder why it seems so dark
out there
I felt the earth quake
I feel it start again
and I could swear I heard my grandfather's voice
he was a rabbi too
Heaven and earth feel as desolate as I.

PETER ON PENTECOST
(Acts 2:22-38)

I'm listening Peter,
for you speak of what I'd like to see,
And you have seen,
and then were sent
with force beyond all meter
to convince the likes of me,
so sick of what has been.

Jesus the Nazarene!
Tell me of him; make me wonder;
what God has done through him
and what he meant
to all of you who heard the thunder
of his voice, and learnt to swim
the flood, held by his hand unseen.

On purpose God delivered him
for men to crucify.
He died. Pagans did it,
but could not hold him down.
Now I know why
David was glad and sung hymn after hymn
Knowing his treasure would stay where he had hid it;

For evermore upon his throne
His favorite son will sit

He witnessed it,
he sees the uncreated crown
rest on the head which he had known
which thorns, like fire, had lit
and he had wept a bit.

Already, though, King David knew
injustice would not have the day
forever.

From Bethlehem, a little town,
the pilgrim came to fight and slay
the forces that had blocked our view.
Now never.

MEDITATION ON MARK 13

In the presence of the Romans, flee
when greed and pride, ambition, stalks my soul
call me to thee
on some mountain
surely thy heart will answer me.

Keep me on guard, or rather guard me
with thy mind, speak what thou willst
the living ringing Word
singing joy and strength
clear light, though all else
is darkness, warm fire in yearlong winter,
who cares?—when thou art here.

Come in the clouds of prayer and pain
be glory, smile
let me be a child again
in joy, God without guile,
in my vision peace.
Despatch thine angels to make friends with me
let me meet an angel, two or three,
and listen to them teach.

END MY FIGHT

(Isaiah 54:4-10)

O why remember, why not forget, and leave obliterated
what was subtracted?
Why carry over the memory of the rides, the walks,
The eyes that scintillated?
For nothing in the end has been contracted,
And silence came to finish all our talks.
And having said farewell,
Let some one else join me at the altar,
No other than my Maker.
Lead me from my cell
And make me vault a
Prison wall, my own imagination,
Rushing to the strong arms of my God.
You have decreed it,
It was your will,
That you should love this piece of England's sod.
O may you seed it
With grain divine. And take the chill
Exchanging it with sunlight
And holy tears
In showers
After many years
Of dry darkness. End my fight
With peace, and from my dusty sand bring flowers.

FIFTIETH BIRTHDAY

The stillness of a winter dawn
lamps and trees like lines of unemployed
aged and forlorn
but for one loyal bird
singing as they beg some warm
bread, some seed or leaves, some light.
They sing the end of night.

Evening now,
the day is past and present.
It has seen its laughter,
but what remains
is just the hour of truth
when we spoke of you,
the rosary,
and heaven, now.

I ran two miles
and half a century had ticked away.
But the beam was carried in my eye.
I asked for healing
and you gave me repose.

EVERYONE LONELY*
(to Chiara)

Through you he has touched me here
made me see his plan
on his old foundation prayer
can be sad for every man
and you will turn that sorrow
into joy tomorrow
when we're not alone
but he stands upon my stone.

That morning there'll be what to share
secret love in verse
fruit of all the pain and tears
that do not rhyme but worse
than eros tear the heart apart
and give the spirit just a start
to paradise, much more than fun
where even I in him with you'll be One.

Thunder now and hail
a hurricane of fear
upon my raft lift up a sail
and hold the tiller dear
you've set a light upon the shore
a light which was our peace before
and under night's majestic dome
I'll find my altar home.

*This is a response to the meditation entitled "Everyone who is lonely" in the book *Meditations* by Chiara Lubich (London: New City Press, 1971, page 24)

TO SAINT MARIA GORETTI

If I have tied my boat to hers
Perhaps I'll not go down
I shall not surely drown
But by her brilliant eyes be steered
Though I am blind
Past all I've feared
All flooded dikes and weirs
And hidden snares
Of every kind
Below the river or above
Of mountain gale or ocean wave
She'll save me with her prayers
Her love
From any grimy grave
That I so foolishly have dug
'Neath every wave my oarsmen slug
With lazy, angry, blinded stroke.
If I am still, and tie my boat
To hers, I'll surely not go down
I surely shall not drown.

Batter that breeze
Dash the waves
Steer me steer me on
It's not with ease

That courage braves
These storms, but steer me on
Twilight or dawn
Hope forlorn
Wind fling fear upon
The haughty storm
And chloroform
The pride that beats it on;
Terrify
The raging sky
Cry my saint's aboard!
The rock-bound cliff-high harbor looms
The city of the Lord.

THE CATCH

No one, because
They each will pause
Looking only for You;
When he sees
Some other grinning face
Or frowning, each flees
Knowing nothing will do
Without Your grace.

In her they found You.
I too;
October find.
Do You mind
If I now sit or kneel
And weep for joy?
So long although
Ago
I took that meal
And only ate the peel
As though it were a toy.

MY NIGHT KNOWS NO DARKNESS

Chiara speaks:
My nights are never dark
My pain is joy
My night is God is Light
My pain is His, is Love
Just for the world;
Sleepless, by many thousands followed, I walk
A field, where once was sand.

Julian speaks:
My days are nights
because your word is light
and if I cannot hear
your music in my inner ear
how can I find my way
or know what I'm to say
to fellow or to you or self itself?
It's dark today.

Christ speaks:
Your darkness cannot overcome my word,
It's stronger than the gloom of fall
And warmer than your icy, empty soul.
Despite you I will conquer and be heard.
Come to my nocturnal music, youth,
Come where the living leaves are stirred,
Be wafted high, higher than the highest uncouth
Faker of my incomparable word.

DESERT STARS

The stars are close, in the desert.
I do not care
       to shuffle 'long the bed of dried-up rivers
       under the desert sun.
But the stars at night are a dazzling hope
       that Heaven is close
       when all is done.

Lights shine brightest in the dark
But do not burn.

Orioles, quail, and pairs of wrens
Sing from joshua trees, and under shrubs
       in the desert sun.
But under the stars
       we hear You best. The silence gets attention—
       one by one—
For every word by every star that's spoken.
Listen: "God is love."

THE SUMMER LONG

Throw back your head in the sun
Roll it back that the Creator may caress you
He alone, of others none
Do you need, let Him come because He loves to.

Smile the summer long
The sunshine's fingers through your golden hair
The summer songbirds' song
Ringing, singing in your ear!

Around the world pure will be the air,
Clear the light, beautiful the soft sound
For you are here like a lamp in a sanctuary
An organ-pipe sweet and clear.

LOOK FORWARD

I look forward to the day
When God will set me free
From the wheels of routine
That turn with heartless speed along the road to death,

To the cessation
Of movement
When the brakes of time will grip the asphalt.

I look forward to the cessation
Of the grinding of the wheels
And the rolling of axles
And the fleeting of moments,
The silence when even the sun stands still,

Not even the endless hush and hiss
Of the ocean waves
Will disturb the celestial music of the stars.

Stars, sing me your silent psalm
Let me sleep in your song.

Still night of eternity
Breathe a sigh.
I long to sleep in the sky,
To lie where there is peace with no wheels.

TOUCH

People were bringing their little children to Him to have Him touch them.   Mark 10:13

If You would touch a child
He'd not forget,
You smiled,
And he'd remember.
More than met,
He'd felt
God in the wild.

Like in September
The winter's touch,
Tho' mild,
Is sure, in frosts;
The grown-up child,
In woolen blankets piled
Will now look back
To what he's lost
And feel the lack,
But long at any cost
To grasp Your Godhead undefiled
Forever. The Spring is such
A joy to hope for, past December.

RELEASE

Jubilation, jubilee!
Sudden light has set us free
From the tunnels of the dark,
From the choking coal dust. Hark,
Hist the sifting of the breeze
Through the leaves of green old trees;
See the sunlight in the pale
Evening of the western vale;
Watch the mist from streamlets rise,
Lofty clouds across the skies
From east to west their showers bring
To fertile plain and plants that cling
Below our feet to mountains steep,
Where our poor shepherds watch our sheep.
Jubilation, jubilee!
Never thought that we should see
Our native hills again, or breathe
The passion their strong airs unsheathe.
Jubilation, jubilee!
To God the Father glory be.

Maryland

MARYLAND

Earth has its heaven, its home,
For me the land split like my heart
    around the glassy bay,
For me the fields of twelve-foot corn,
Where the buzzards swarm at woods-edge,
And the molten lead of the weekday sun.
Let your black children sing your paeans
    to the cloudless sky,
Let the kingfishers fly
Where the wind blows gently
In the sumac at river's edge.
Sweet red earth, seeded with heaven's song.

"CONFITEOR"

When I was a bluejean kid
Footing Kentucky field path dust
The colors were sunlight green in the world
Summer sky blue
My song was a lung laugh
With face in the sun and eyes closed
The birds sang a lovelier song
Sang it to death
Happy death in earth's forgetfulness.
Bare branches of apple trees
Where your feathers imperceptibly trembled
And fell to the ground in agony
Violin strings of earth's trees' root joy broken.
O bare branches of apple trees
I saw you in fat fruit green in sheep-shade
I loved you in that hour with your redwing blackbirds
That chanted my confiteor.

HOWARD COUNTY

Beyond the hunter's tread I heard
A dove, yet no shot followed
For the autumn mists are heavy
The dogwoods and locusts and wild cherry
In full leaf. Behind the corn shocks
That shine from last summer's sunlight
Against the woods' gold, green, and black, and red,
A crow flies low to the ground,
And children's voices came from a stream
In the ox-woods, the whole county smiled,
Sang for a moment:
An oriole on Waters Hill,
Its voice is dying, but its echoes
Have come,
        have come,
                have come.

WINTER SUN

It's winter now and yet the chilly sun
Gives some idea across the pale blue sky
Of harvest time and joy of death
After the lusts of spring
The luscious sprouting of the clover fields
The ground hogs' feed,
And the blossom time the honey time
The revelling of the bees
Buzzing in the crickets' song
Weaving in green grasshoppers' dance
In the August breeze.
It's winter now, time of expectation
Short days between long nights of toil.
Toil on winter, come harvest time and scythe,
Come on death, gathered in the Father's barn.

SHALL I KILL?

The afternoon is pressing low with heat
My day's work in the woods is done,
I have leant the scythe against the garage wall
And taken my rifle, slung
Over my shoulder, and up the hill I walk
Out of the trees;
The sun is hot and the sweat stings
In my eyes,
The clay is red in the field
And to my side off over the field
All that I love walks with her head bowed
And her dog alone.
Up through the heat over the hill the question burns:
　　　Shall I kill this life? Shall I kill?

WHY ARE YOU SAD?

Why am I sad? it is because the corn is green.
And what I have heard: it is the sound of crickets in the hay.
And what I have seen:
The poplars and the locusts in the day,
And night time lightning bugs lighting up the green.
　Though all the years did fly,
　Still, her hair is brown, her laugh the same, her way,
　Her every way the same, increased and charged.
—Would that I might die.

SONG OF THE WORLD

I love a friend
A steep green climbing hill
Tulip poplars, oaks, and elms,
And locust trees,
And in the spring the dogwood bloom
I love the world

I love the springs
The streams,
The rivers, and the eagles soaring down,
The hawks, and owls that noiselessly
Glide between the maple leaves
To hunt the timid prey
I love the blood that bathes the earth
The frightened cry of death and sacrifice

I love the fighting bird
The gamecock in his tartan and his spurs
And I have heard
The jaybird cry alarm
And the sun drink in
The weeda-weeda bird, his song,
The red-eyed vireo singing
While he hunts his insect food.

I love the world.
    It sings.

THE VISION

The pollen from the apple blossoms blows
   through your chestnut hair
The scent from the apple blossoms does not trouble me
As the scent from your chestnut hair
Recalling a life, a vision, beyond the squirrel woods
And the groundhogs' haunts in the clover pasture.

What...What...
What wind stirred your plaided skirts?
And stabbed me between the ribs
With a sickening longing for a life in the sun,
Out there beyond the loveliness
Where the crow swerves in his lonesome flight.

With you I am lonely, as a mateless crow in winter flying
From Rockburn up the river
Seeking for the life beyond the valley, the hills,
   the beeches and the firs;
The vision recalled in light.

The vision's in your eyes
Like a great central fire, that glows in smiles
Meeting the seer in dirty streets
In the German chords of a forest early morning.
The vision pipes death beyond life
From a cardinal's beak in a hot evening.

EVOCATION

Look down the hill at the rest of your childhood
Where are the years of dogwood in bloom?
Over the rocks flows the cold clear water
Your beautiful maid met you last at her tomb
The sun casts its beams alone through the oaktrees
Up in the treetops the squirrels flee doom
Across the front field the crack of a rifle
And later in darkness the owls cried, "For whom?"

IN A EUROPEAN CITY

I hear no frogs singing, though it's springtime
And I wish I were again standing
In the sodden red clay of my friends' pasture,
Looking through the blue mist slight under a May sun
At the woods along Rockburn,
Listening to the song of frogs under the locust trees
    and honeysuckle,
Dreaming of a smile I love
And eyes I never see without a thrilling pain;
Sad I used to stand there, with a rifle under my arm,
And a buzzard clumsily soaring over the trees.

England

WELLS CATHEDRAL

Slowly round the towers curves the sky
Slowly reaches round the sun to shine
Warmthless but lightsome gold upon the rock
Near the end of time

Shimmer lake weep eyes
Out around the pile
Inside the Word shines in through bits of glass
Deeptoned syllables of chanting light
For ears to hear
And the church shines with the glory of the fishermen
   and the sun
Until the end of time.

DARTMOOR HYMN

Open my lips with the key of Thy mercy
And I shall praise Thee for the driving rain
Praised be Thy handiwork in the bogs of the moorland
Blessed in heather and the bracken terrain
Praised be Thy Word in song of the skylarks
Blessed be He in the song of Thy streams
Praised in the sheep, praised in the ravens
Harsh chords in His jubilee
Praised be Thy Spirit in the wind of the tor-tops
Praised in the ponies that canter the lea
Here by the riverside: praised be the Holy Trinity.

THE HIGH LANDS

Breathe the air for there is nothing else
The ground is high the wind
Is gentle, cold the air and light
The deer are distant, only they
Accompany this far the wandering man.
Far below the village with its loves
Live in their smoke now lost to sight
O silent peace O wind, what of the night
Up in the snows to which I grow more near
What of the rocks the melting streams below
What company will be there? None
But the crinkling snows and the God of it all
There near He dwells where no one goes
Until he has died in the snows.

74

LOCH NESS

Here the seagull soars
Here the rain pours, and the wind
Blows impatient clouds along the highlands
And draws long-reaching ribbons
Of white along the waves.
Here the drenched deer
Waits for the rifle
And stares across the great glen
With tragic face of fear.

RAIN IN SCOTLAND

After the roaring winds the clouds have fallen
Down the hills, and met again in streams
That tumble on in unthinking childhood,
Mature, and join in rivers
Through fearsome chasms and wicked rapids
Distracted, savage, glum
To empty in a lake
And wake
Surprised, to the peaceful blue and the gentle clouds
And the golden sun, mirrored from above.
So the soul comes to the late season of love.

OXFORD RAIN

Sorrow came over the spires
In the rain
In my beginning
From the Berkshire downs
And the sweep of the ocean
Beyond the beginning

Here was I compounded
Of the mists, and the powdery rain
Rising from the cobbles
And November pregnant rivers

Here was my beginning
But from beyond
Came the rain
With an aspiration

GALE IN THE COTSWOLDS

Sway, golden heads,
spread waves of corn
and leaves in forest undulation.
Bright clouds of cumulus
like oceanic breakers
pound the brilliant sky
offending the sun itself
with titanic
courage and skill,
billowing round
from our tiny globe,
pressing it back,
back to its fearful hole,
locked in thunderous contest
sun and cloud
till the end of the beginning of time.

MY MOTHER'S FUNERAL

Grief unutterable
to recall:
clear Autumn morning
when after due warning
Heaven took Earth
in a pall.

MY BROTHER'S FUNERAL

"God be with you" 's my good-bye
Crying up the valley of the Wye
Knowing you are now with God
At the foot of Penyard, under Ross' sod
Where you walked your little life
Eternally a child,
Gentle and mild,
You shall come to no harm
For you did none, caused no alarm.
Pass from my love into His
Which is the same, unmediated,
    Father's and Brother's kiss.

"PROSPECT HILL"
(Ross-on-Wye)
to my parents

Now we understand
On Prospect Hill
What the English land
Is speaking still:

Words we could not say
Thoughts we could not find,
While the timid day
Of earth could bind.

With dawn-ray's thrust
Heaven between us three,
Made brave with trust,
Shall set us free.

CLIFTON HAMPDEN*

Through greenbanked willow streams
Let Thames meander
Fed by childhood dreams
And swept by snowwhite swans

Memories of goose and gander
Swim with duckling teams
In v-formation yonder

And while I ponder
This scene of a life that's gone
Back to the age-old bridge I wander
And Thames beneath flows proudly on.

*"My" village, where my home in England was, eight miles down the Thames from Oxford.

SANDFORD*

Fling your rain West Wind
    Across the groggy ground
    Fling your gale.
The earth bespattered spongelike with your ire,
    Pummeled with your hail,
    Shivers eastward and reels around,
    Cannot stand your fire.
Fling your fury shout and cry that we have sinned.
Soaked with your rain, I love you in my native sod,
Ride into you and laugh and sing, for you're the voice of God.

*A village on Henley Road, near Oxford

THE GOVERNESS
(Monica Katherine Tottie)

From some golden flowers make her a crown,
Let their rays shine into infinity.
Set it where tears once fell in showers
And there had been a frown.
(The fault was mine.) The Trinity,
Beyond compare, and uncreated Powers
Shall be her gown,
Surrounded by the children
Who grew, like grapes on a vine,
Or round a little wren
Her egg-fruit, or towers
Ring a mountain town.
She was strong
In discipline and love,
And like from grapes strong wine
Flowed wisdom as her dowers,
And raised above
All in the throng she met
Who had been down.
They weave for Tots an everlasting crown
And set it on her brow to shine.

ROBERTS*

On the stairs a shy farewell
In the turning of the stairs embarrassment
Time has brought no understanding only
A brief shy reunion on the sombre turning
Of the stairs. Before the final separation,
Farewell.

Now I return, the trees are turning,
Workmen clean the blackened stone,
I try not, cannot reach you on the phone,
And even now the setting sun is burning:
Farewell.

*The Vice Provost of Worcester College, a fine old gentleman, who had
died by the time I went up to St Benet's Hall.

GOODBYE TO AN ENGLISH MONK

The ocean waves to you are good-bye in my name
The ocean calls and flings farewell
On the shouldering cliff-foot rocks.
Listen. Catch the spray in your hair,
For the ocean's cry, the smoke on the evening sky,
The lashing wind, and I
Will die, leaving the starlight
Stabbing silence through your eye.

MORNING MASS

Here to St Giles
Calvary came in springtime
At an early hour
When the blackbirds and the Thief and I
Said one Latin Creed
The dawn spoke to the dawn:
I believe.

PUSEY LANE

Cry to the night
To the gaslight
After the rain

What shall I cry
Farewell, goodbye
I leave you, with your pain

The Lord be with you
And in your hour, again
Tread in this cobble lane
And rain His faith within you.

FALL EVENING

Sometimes I light my pipe and the fall evenings are long
And getting cool, gone the summer song,
Somehow my mind returns
My mind and heart and lungs long to return
To the Studio fireside, to Van and Jean,
To the maroon armchair, sinking there
We will talk of prayer,
And the gaslight and perhaps the evening rain
Will rise in mist from the lane,
As our wills to God to mortal eyes unseen.

TO JEAN VANAUKEN*

In the valley where the creeks run dry
Plant this my cross, hold it before your eye
The sap that flows from the wounded side
Of this tree's fruit, our Savior Christ, Who died
That you might live, will stream to you
   with life that cannot die.

In the valley where this world's lights won't shine
Look at the mother moon and the sun divine
On this dark wood. And from their two pierced hearts
Let light come in that counterparts
The sorrow and the joy in your two hearts and mine.

*This refers to a wooden cross, 7 inches high, which I sent Jean when she was dying. It is old, I don't know where it came from, Germany probably. It was given me by Evelyn Harrison, an old friend of my father's in Baltimore. At the top is a figure of God the Father, blessing the world. Between the Father and the Crucified is a dove, representing the Holy Spirit. At the foot of the cross is Mary, holding her hand over her heart, which is pierced by a sword descending over her left shoulder (in fulfilment of Simeon's prophecy).

AH STUDIO!

(On reading the manuscript of the Oxford chapters of
A Severe Mercy*)*

Ah Studio! We'll meet again.
It won't be gaslight in the lane,
But just as gentle, only brighter.
And Jack on Aslan's back.
We'll sing His glory
Around those two: One Love-truth
Old World will give one final 'crack!'
Our hearts could not be lighter.

ON READING
'A SEVERE MERCY'

O triumph! I've waited long
Through grey wastepaper days
Through cigarettes and emptied glasses
Hearing only a single sparrow's song
—Poor piper, for Davy's death—
Turning now to my student lasses
Praying someone will love them too
Now I dare to believe God's ways
Contain such unforeseen mercies
As Davy's resurrection, through
A book that breathes her breath,
The faith and love in our undying verses.

DOWNSIDE

Downside has my heart
enwombed
in the white arches.
That organ plays
my guardian angels' praise
to God.

A red cross on gold,
the colours and the bunting fly
above the school
and friendships which will last,
many, forever.

"I love it here,"
is my repeated prayer.
I love it here.
It must not be an idol, though.
Let only God be dear.

Watch over me, God of Downside,
for I have no one else
as ground to hold me,
arms to enfold me
on this, the first day of Your life.

In the darkness of my mind
You will find
me watching still,
for Your Will.

Rome

GOD ON THE AVENTINE

Down the channels of the ocean through the storm
Down the rain-varnished streets, the streets of Rome
Through the alleys of the ghetto to the Aventine
Through lecture rooms
Through choir
Through the study hour
Red-eyed your lids with desire
Red-eyed with weeping and with fire
Your Holy Spirit in my cell of stone
Echoed Its cry I could not hear
I could not condone
Could I lie down upon the bed of prayer
And cast away stretched out there
The reputation to which I aspire
Could I stand the holy furnace of the choir?

VIA SAN TEODORO

These images loom in stone
The latin sun is there again
Above the Palatine and this road,
The past, come to console,
To recall past friendship and past pain
And to suffer beneath the pine trees again
The agony of the sunlight on old ruined brick
And the bliss of loneliness, of history, and emptiness
O my God, where shall we meet again?

SUNRISE ON ROME

Spearshafts of gold on the green dawn sky,
Clouds dressed in rose-purple tatters,
Each minute purple glows more light rose
As the sun nears the arch of dawn,
Best loved of all the Father's creatures.
Swordpoint of sun breaks the edge of the mountain
Shouting a greeting in the sky.
Rose turns to grey, gold to white
Unable to compete
With the spring of light
And father of all color.
The sky from sickly green grows royal blue
And can no longer bear your glare,
Brother Sun, nor gaze at you.

ALBAN SUNSET

I saw the sun go down
Tearing the clouds like shawls from off the mountains
Blushing with laughter before his pale blue mind
That lay behind
Contemplating infinity in a dream of immortality
Scattering desire

The fields were trumpeting
And the sun was drumming on the mountains

I heard the sea
Sighing its sadness far away
The gulls like violins wailed in sorrow
For the meaningless end of day
And the sun was falling laughing
While the night crept in with him
To stay.

ROMAN LAD

I saw a boy swimming in the Tiber
The loin cloth clung cotton to his body
White limbs and the muddy river
Sapling limbs climbing from the moving water
Rome's eyes looked with a mother's pleasure.

SANT'ANSELMO EVENING

I thought the bell pealed out again, cruel,
Bricked up within the smooth complacent tower
I thought the darkness fell
The trams were clanging
And the emptiness hung like cloud
Around the window
Reaching sifting through the corridor to
Empty all but memory from the mind.

IL FIGLIUOLO CHE SORRIDE*

Come down the stairs
And smile
Always smile
And let your open neck
Be hot
And clammy
In the weather
I will not touch you
I will go by
But I will weep.

I want you
Always, always
To come down the stairs
Smiling
Eternally smiling
And in your eternity
Without touching
I will go by
Weeping.

*Literally, the title is Italian for "The Son Who Smiles"; it was
intended as a counterpart to T.S. Eliot's "La Figlia Che Piange" (The
Daugher Who Weeps).

DAY AT ANTICOLI

Did You spread out that valley for *me*?
So in the spring-green checkerboard I might see
Your enamouring Beauty kaleidoscoped and hear
That stream, the echo of that Gloria
Sung this week by the reborn in our land,
Where I am not.
                              Here in my middle way
Is my beginning, where my father* student-eyed and wondering
Walked with trembling fearlessness up Anio's stream.
"Before Anticoli stacked its homes, Amen," You say to me,
"I was." Before the Arab peasant ploughed Your glory in
        that dale
You found a cave for me. Where a candle burns of hope
Farther down the earthly way.

*The "father" referred to here is St Benedict, who must have walked
this way, when he left the life of a student in Rome for the cave in
Subiaco up-stream.

96

OSTIA IN JUNE

Let the sea break
Unrelenting
On the crumbling ridge of sand,
Let the latin sun
Bake the sandy shore
To scorch my feet
And beat the blue sea to a lovelike color.
O the wind, my loved one,
The wind
Blows the sand into my eyes.

Would the blue sea storm us sandwards
In collision
Would the sun scorch savage in our perdition
Let us at last reach Godwards in submission
Let us fling our souls
Windlike
Down the vision.

Rhode Island

LAMB OF GOD

In the silence of the sea
a new moon was the lamb of God
that takes away the darkness of the world.
It was the most high
where, like polished slate, the smooth and silent water
nursed its gulls till dawn.

STILLNESS

A tiny gust of wind stirs the twigs
Above the snow
And melting ice from them drops slow
Into the brush beneath

If creation weeps in this still hour
Like it is bleak depressed in mood and quiet
What of You Lord God because
We wander lost in Your despite
Here apart?

CROWS ON THE EVENING SKY

Crows in the winter sky
Flying westward flying high
The sound of shotguns makes them shy
Crows in the evening light
Pinkish pale of vast height
Before the dazzling stars of night
Crows in the falling day
Pinheads black, high on their way
At early dusk the owls' sweet prey
Crows in the falling day.

FEBRUARY

Grey bitter wind
Of roaring season
Flaying the earth snow-skinned
Visiting treason.
The chestnuts wait with calm,
Blackened and beaten.

> Not long till the days of palm,
> Till the Supper's eaten;
> Not long till the spring has come,
> Till the sun is risen
> To free the leaf from gloom
> And the heart from prison.

AUGUST DAWN

The light approaching praises You
the brutes of night are crawling home
land and sea birds stir their song
again the time is come
to heed Your call
"Rejoice, adore the martyrs' King"
sift the darkness through the earth
and let the glory in unseen.

AUGUST MORNING

I walked a quarter mile down to a pond
The sheep rose from their beds, riled
    but without a sound
I looked at apples rotting wild
    upon the ground
And hoped for all the death that lay beyond.

OCTOBER HUNTING

Over the fullrunning streams burbling
   through the marsh
Deep dark grey was the low heaven, swift in the wind,
Yellow-brown the woods, color of sand, the end of fall
And all was rain and winter tearing in.
Last of October, gone the harvest and the fruits,
   to cellar and silo,
Gone the slim shirtsleeved weeks, come the months
   of hunting
Hot pursuit of frightened pheasant, fox and cottontail
In the freezing breeze, stripping leaves from cover,
   cold death to crittur
Below the dark swiftmoving sky that night
   is quickly overtaking.
Starry night of end of fall, starry night of winter,
Woken by the sound of geese, flying to their shelter,
Man and sheep shall meet you in his clothes of wool,
   lights burning,
Who but night shall keep
The crittur till the morning?

NARRAGANSETT FALL

North Wind over the sea
paints the leaves in oils
red, russet, and gold.
Forty times now I have seen
leaves fallen and old.
And I believe in the North Wind
who trails white foam
while striding the gridiron of the sea,
all arctic and cold.

The North Wind had the mists in his coils
the moon and stars came out and grinned
and took green summer home.

NOVEMBER

Drip the rain
Drip drip November
Drip again
Chuck chuck the robin
Chuck the thrush, the sparrow
Autumn with his bow and arrow
Has shot the leaves with a redeeming pain
Shot the trees with gold
The earthly sky is sobbing
For no such eye can still remember
A death so noble, dying with such gain
It is not old
But new, this summer's ember.

105

WILD WEDNESDAY

Wild Wednesday
when the wind
sent the student
all hair-blown
surprised but smiling

Wild teeming rain
on the courts
windows banging in the wind
which whistled
with despair in the air

Nothing accomplished
only the student
brought his poem
wide-eyed and smiling
and the wind behind him

Wild Wednesday and this rain
will not fall this way again.

NOTHING CAN REMAIN

Are there words that could express this yearning
These tears, a nor'easter blowing?

Eyes lift up through the wind-driven rain
The dark afternoon of fall,
When summer morning has died from recollection
And the love of spring lives still
Sadly.

When the leaves were green, we loved them,
And we listened to the woodpecker in the elm tree
When the leaves reflected back the sun's own music
In a thousand blades of light.
How young the spring was,
And how hot the day, the June-time of our lives.

But today, in the reds and golds of autumn
Cold and drab, in the northeastern rain, ocean rain,
Nothing can remain but to call goodbye
Be still in love and die.

THE WHITE OAK

Stand still, white oak
I do not need
To beg you, white oak, to stand still
While the copper beech beneath
Bounces, like the waves
Of the sea.
Keep still, white oak.
I do not need
To beg you forever
To stand still.

Stand still, white oak.
I do not need
To beg you, white oak, to stand still
While the silver birch
Sways in its somnambulistic dance,
Twinkling its early leaves.
Keep ever still, white oak,
Everlastingly.
I do not need, white oak,
To implore that forever
You be still.

THE TIDE

What was the seagull thinking
When the tide came in on the stone
On which he sat and pondered
One of his dreams?
Where did he go when he flew
With the chain of his dream disturbed
'Way round the point up the shore?
The sea came in just the same
Line after line of waves
Higher so high on the rocks,
Grew still, and ebbed again,
Leaving a fresh green seaweed line
And froth on the pebbles and shale.
The old gull drifted over the coast
Down on his rock, whinnied and screamed
And resumed his dream,
When the air was salty and hot and still.

POINT JUDITH

For the bent old men that walk white-haired to the sea,
For the white horses, beyond the surf,
For the terns, the gulls and the echo of their cries,
And for the swan, I thank You, Lord.

For the nets and the ships and the harvest they reap,
For the fear of the ocean and the courage of men who sail,
For the long nights shrouded in cloud and tossed under spray,
And raining wind, I thank You, Lord.

For the odor of clam and lobster,
For the sifting sound of the wake of a sailboat,
For the pounding of the waves, the throbbing motors,
And the ruffling flags, I thank You, Lord.

For the tribes that fished here, aeons ago,
And vanished, for the rich that possessed their land,
For the unseen who are yet to come and be born,
And will fish here, I thank You, Lord.

For the joy of the autumn sun and its setting,
For the winter yet to come, driving settlers away,
For the geese and wild duck that the spring will follow,
And the world of the ocean, I praise You, Lord.

EASTER IN NEWPORT

Who now believes in Thee?
The sailboats harbored on the sea?
Do the rest crucify
Or just indifferently ride by?

O Wisdom, the earth is bored at you
Mankind is bitter at your joy
But at Saint Spyridon they bring
You flowers, sing your Mother's lamentation
May every generation
Sing in sorrow for your wrong,
In triumph, for you've conquered us
Our sin, our pain, our heart.

Women come, young girls with myrrh
And make your body scent the air
A hundred candles show our faith
With light from light of Easter;

Dispel our dark,
O light that burned beneath the ground
O life now dead, O stream that stopped,
The road nowhere at an end.

Afterthoughts

GRACE AND PEACE
a meditation on 2 Peter

2 Pt. 1:1-2   Why should the mist
seem to bring peace
more than the sun on the sea?
When the waves hissed,
angered like geese,
sunlight seemed hostile to me.
Somerset green
fathers my prayer,
rooks in the morning seem calm.
Swans of the queen
gracefully bear
peace to our nature, and balm.

1 Pt. 1:2-3   Faith in the Saviour
shared with apostles
brings us a goodness divine.
He who forgave your
refuge in fossils
offers a new life to mine.
Drawn by the glory
powerful virtue
throws in our scandalized eyes,
hark to the story
which never hurt you,
which the evangelist cries.

2 Pt. 1:3-4   Promise me joy,
knowledge of You,
I can leave women behind.
Once to a boy
glimpses came through:
Thunder had lightened my mind.

2 Pt. 1:5-8   Holiness comes
after the light
virtue engenders in man.
Holiness plumbs
deep in the white
light where the Crossbearer ran.
Gift of the light
sings. Moonlight hums.
Clearly O Spirit we can
listen to bright
tones that our ignorance ban.

2 Pt. 1:9-10   Let me remember
horrors of shame,
boredom, and bitter despair
come with December;
losing my name,
groping for guiderails, a stair,
anything, raising me
out of the dark
swamp at the foot of the hill,
lightning amazing me
fleeing the bark
driving my heels to your will.

116

2 Pt. 1:11   Up to the summit
              where we're alone
              up to the realm of your love.
              Sing it or hum it,
              "Sanctus" is flown
              winged on the voices above:
              Seraphim sing it,
              Cherubim hum,
              man on his cross is the drum
              marching, to bring it
              skywards, to come
              into the song of the dumb,
              light of the blind,
              life of the dead.
              Strumming your victory song,
              losing we find,
              fasting we're fed,
              falling we stumble along.

2 Pt. 1:12-14   God never fails.
                 Man never wins.
                 God will be all we can have.
                 Biblical tales,
                 dreams held by pins,
                 such will be all we can save.
                 Every ship sails
                 back into port
                 (thought she had left it behind).
                 End of the rails,
                 we shall be caught
                 right where our metal was mined.

2 Pt. 1:15-16   Back to the past,
forward to God,
both are the same in the end;
truth has to last;
bean in a pod
grows to a vine we can tend,
ends in the same
species of bean
multiplied over the days,
days of no game,
bent in our lean
labor beneath the sun's rays:
sunlight and rain
bow the man down
prostrate, before weather's King;
slow comes the gain:
after the frown,
birdlike, the harvesters sing.

2 Pt. 1:17-21   Honour and glory
need we now bring You?
Just let us see what You are.
Harvest the story
where we can ring You
round Your new altar, not far:
down in the choir
let us now hear
voices of Father and Son.
Otherwise higher
into the clear
light of the biblical sun.
Into the dark

came a new fire
where the Three Flames coinhere.
Up like a lark
prayers aspire
singing their song all the year.

Once on a mountain
Peter could see You
shine like a star come to earth.
You are the fountain
light-thirst can flee to,
giving the sunshine its birth.
Sun in the heart
set in a cloudless
sky, cleansed with water and fire;
tears are our part
shed in a boundless
lake You reclaimed from the mire.

2 Pt. 2:1-8   Water of joy
as we give thanks
reading your prophets and saints;
sad we annoy,
childish with pranks,
even ourselves with our taints,
2 Pt. 2:8-22   vexing our souls
which have betrayed
secrets You gave us to keep,
fearing the coals
justice has laid
where the impure cannot sleep.
Govern our wills
humble our minds

steer us along the right way,
round the green hills
where the path winds
over the grass and the clay.
Gorges we'll pass,
storms in the day,
darkness will not get us lost;
only alas
money may weigh
heavily, more than the cost
needed to pay
interest at least
towards the great debt that is owed.
Giving away
blood for our feast
sure You deserve what You've sowed:
life in our veins
thoughts in our minds
love from our hearts, never cold.
You take the reins.
Grace, then, unbinds
knots in the prayers You unfold.

2 Pt. 3   Saved from the dark,
slaves to no lust,
free to devote life to You;
always remark,
coming You must
free us from all that we do.
Free us for prayer
fleeing the fire,
after a thousand more years—

now, if we care
now to aspire
after the Son as He nears.

Word of the Father
made the green earth
crisscrossed with rivers and streams,
watered with rather
delicate mirth,
showers and mist, and the beams
down from the clouds
over the hills,
searchlights of sunshine between,
2 Pt. 3:4   into the crowds,
healing our ills,
showing a path that is clean
straight to His Will,
always in sight
gazing on Him in our midst.
Always You fill
people with light,
people who pray, "Lord thou didst
ever command...",
people who say
"Thank You, because You have come."
What You demand
is that we stay,
whether we speak or are dumb,
true to our ray
—the light of Your Will—
to the commandment of love.
Every new day

121

sunny or chill
leads from our cross up above.

2 Pt. 3:6 World of the past
perished except
moments eternal: like prayer,
visions that last,
beauty that leapt
up in our eyes. Let us dare
reach for some more
visions of God
leaving the wooden alone;
snow will all thaw
showing the sod
soft to our flesh and our bone.

2 Pt. 3:7 Fire will burn
them away too:
all of our letters and books.
Now let me turn
only to You,
fire or nature like hooks
which You can use,
Fisher of souls,
catching Your most willing prey;
saints can enthuse
fish, for the bowls
where You'll consume us one day.

2 Pt. 3:13 Life will be new
earth will be too,
sky, and the whole universe,
whether we're few

only with You,
all, or just many—but worse
far would be if
I am not there,
caught in my lust and my pride.
Back from the cliff
black let me wear,
last let my place be. But slide
not into sin.
Save me one thing.
Save me Your Self, That's enough.
Better has been
nothing to sing,
nor any time spent, than tough
hours in the church
praying, or walks
talking and listening to You,
2 Pt. 3:14   loving to search
woodlands, and talks,
writing, or art of the few
silent and calm
saints of the past:
forests and woods of the soul
whisp'ring a psalm
breathing the vast
yearning of heart for the coal
burning in heaven,
glowing in churches,
hiding in nature's old veil,
hiding its leaven
back of the perches
where the birds sleep through the gale

123

tearing our days
off from the rails
laid through the quiet woods of prayer,
setting ablaze
passion, that jails
faith in a prison of fear.

2 Pt. 3:15-18   Patience of Christ
cure our disease,
bind us to You with a vow.
We've sacrificed
self, with the keys
given to Peter for now.
Firm in the breeze
steadfast in storms
praying You still them. Let's grow
great on our knees,
escaping the worms,
faithful until we can know.

(finished August 6, 1978, the day of the death of Pope Paul VI, r.i.p.)

YOUR MERCIES

(a meditation on Psalm 89)

verses

1-4   I'll sing till I'm hoarse of Your mercies,
I'll watch generations pass by
In vanity, writing their verses,
And singing their songs on the sky,
In emptiness building their castles
And laying on sand brittle bricks,
In murder and fraud and in hassles
For wages and taxes and kicks.
I'll launch my canoe on the waters
Of truth that gush forth from Your side.
I'll paddle upstream how You taught us
With strokes of strong love up the tide,
I'll give You my hand to the covenant,
I'll take to my lips Jesus' cup
Each time I escape from the government
To pause at the bank, or to sup.

5-6   The seed of Your servant has grown now.
Once planted in Mary's pure womb,
He's grown like the fruit of the rowan bough:
Red berries enthroned where there's room:
On altars, in hearts that are emptied
Of selfportrait idols, in priests
Your oil has anointed, though tempted
Like Judas to sell Him at feasts,

125

The skies will yet praise Him tomorrow,
The sun rising over the smog
Will send out its rays red as sorrow
For men who are blind in the fog.

7-8 I'll come to Your Church and I'll listen
To truth from the lips of Your Son
For clouds on the dawn cannot glisten
With glory so strong, only one.
Just one in the history of people
Outshines in His holiness all.
A lighthouse from under the steeple
Shines brighter, for darkness did fall
And tall stands the Teacher transfigured
Above all the prophets and laws.
Like clouds they surround Him who triggered
Explosions of grace in the jaws
Which threatened with greed to devour us,
And cheat us with lies out of life.

8-11 With what will the clouds ever shower us?
With wisdom, where dullness is rife?
Surround us with Truth in a rainstorm
And stir up our hearts for our wife
The Church, and her children, to inform
Them all with the grace of new life
The new revolution of thinking
With faith and humility, free
From storms where our sailship was sinking
In waves of a passionate sea:
My pride beat on walls of reality,
You calmed it with sight of Your face;

126

A word from Your finger, and unity
Came back into focus with grace.

12-13   The skies they are Yours, where the airplanes
Like arrows are shot through the world.
The earth it is Yours, past the sealanes,
Where rivers and forests are curled.
The earth it is Yours, where the mountains
Raise rocks full of prayer through the rain
Up into the sunlight, the fountains
Of warmth, to melt snow on the plain
And fill rocky streams with the torrents
Of thundering, swirling, and bronze
Beneath the white froth, with abhorrence
To frighten the rocks, as if swans
Had beaten their wings in great armies
That swooped on some terrified ducks
And drove them in feathered pajamas
All raucous and squawking with clucks
Like hens who have spotted a falcon—
Thus springtime in flood will release
A force to dislodge what the fall can
Not settle forever in peace.

13-14   You also created the winter,
The endless maze of the seas,
The gales and the storms that can splinter
Our proudest ship's hull, or else squeeze
Her timbers caught in an icepack,
And crucify pride in the cold.
When dying is through, You entice back
To joy and to strength, You enfold

Our spirit in arms of forgiveness
While breathing new love in our lungs,
Humility, tact, sensitiveness.
We climb from our grave up the rungs,
The twelve little steps of St Benet,
Until we can run without fear
Observing by nature the tenet
That You and Your Christ are most dear.

15-16   Your throne, it is shared with the humble,
Your table is shared with the starved,
Your justice and truth start to rumble
(Like thunder where valleys are carved)
In ears that with wealth are complacent
And proud. But around Your stone table
The voices of joy sing out loud,
The hungry are filled, and the stable
Expectant with neighing has vowed
To charge into battle at daybreak
And terrify Satan with prayer,
To press out the wine and to haymake,
To cut and to crush in the glare,
The radiance shed from Your sunlight

17-18   Your face on our back all day long,
Whether we're caught in a gunfight
Or dance in a concert of song.

O God, You're the boast of Your favorite
Who has You, with him, in the midst.
Alone or in crowds he can savor it
That presence of Yours. Thou who didst
Once promise until we have ended
The length of our days on this earth

To stay with the men who have bended
Their knees to give thanks for Your birth.
19-20   You'll raise up our faces to see You
Arrive like the King at our door;
You'll tell us we're wrong if we flee You,
A Father, You've come to the poor
Unlocking such wealth, th'imagination,
Or faith, to believe You've arrived
To help us to feel the sensation
That though we have died, we've survived.

21-22   You've called us to live in Your freedom
As slaves to Your will, not our own,
Anointing our hands, if You need'em
To lift up the gift, not a loan,
Of hearts like a slave's sold forever
Alone to the King of it all;
To play like King David wherever
The Ark and the Cherubim call.
Your hand will help on the zither

And harp, to accompany psalms
And hymns, in the hope you'll come hither
23-24   With grace that delivers and calms.
Like leaves in the fall, our depression,
The moods that harass our soul,
Are driven before a succession
Of winds Your powers control.
Oh calm our distress with Your presence
And rescue our ship from the shoals,
25-26   Lift up our face to the essence
Of sunlight where deep water rolls.
I look on Your face, without trembling

I walk on the cold azure waves;
But when in my heart I'm dissembling
My doubts, or the pride that it craves,
I fall or I sink, and I'm hopeless,
I'm bruised on the rocks where I slip.

27 I call to our Father. There's no less
Than infinite love in His grip.
I cannot believe—but He proves it,

28 He set me where saints, if not kings,
Have stood, on the heights where the spray smit
The ship of apostles, and clings.
Baptismal, refreshing, and sacred
The water like dew from Your grace
Reflecting lights shimmering quake, red
The skin from the wind on our face,

29 But looking on You we are certain
The storms will not smash Peter's ship;

30 For ever and ever we'll skirt then
The shoals where disloyalties slip.
Upon the deep keel we'll be stable
As stars, constellations and sky;
With hand on the tiller we're able
To stay on our feet almost dry.

31-37 And if on the land we should wander
Away from the paths of Your rule
If only in mind we should ponder
Some dark and polluted green pool
In woods uninhabited, shrouding
The briars and the brush from Your sun,
Unhappiness too will be clouding
The joy of the course we had run.

Our prayer will be caught in the tangle
Of creepers and burrs to the waist;
Our work and emotions will wrangle
We're caught in a trap by our haste.
Your mercy will come to our rescue
And reconcile hearts to the truth,
To clear out our ground where distress grew,
That wilderness seeded in youth.
We'll find the true path, where our foot slipped
As if we'd been dropped in a well
Like Joseph, and climb not to Egypt
Nor back to a modern-day hell,
37-38   But into eternal, bright mercy
Enthroned with the humble at rest.
Go forward and leave behind nursie
And all that in childhood was best.

39-40   But where is that mercy, that promise
To answer our prayers, and grant growth?
Or how could a hawk or a crow miss
Locating a tree for them both?
And yet we find that our temple's
Deserted increasingly now;
Our mind, like our clothing unkempt, pulls
Us down like a tree's weary bough.
41   Though fortified once, now we weaken.
There's hardly a youth on our wall
Defending with prayer, like a beacon
To warn off the devils who crawl
Right up to the doors. We are frightened,
Abandoned, it seems, to our death.
For none of our boys are enlightened

With fire like You send with Your breath.
The enemy rattle their motors
Right into our stronghold, and drop
The poisonous gas on our voters
That kills them along with our crop.
A long way away the Dakotas
Prepare for the rescue, perhaps,
To counter the sloth of the lotus
That pins our young men in its wraps.

42-43   And so we've become quite pathetic,
Ridiculous, and a disgrace;
We're old, overweight, not ascetic
Nor brave. We are dull, commonplace.
It seems like the fist of a boxer,
A right hook, were poised for our jaw.
A grin starts to grow, as he knocks a
New victim, he thinks, to the floor.

44-47   You haven't been helping our prayers
You haven't been helping our mind,
Our spirit is senile. Who cares
If we die on the vine unresigned,
Unwashed, and yet spiritually soapless,
Unable to get off the ground,
The dirt where we fell and lie hopeless,
Where only a drunk would be found.
Our days like a weekend are numbered
And spent not in rest but in shame.
We've failed like a look-out who slumbered.
His watery grave bears no name.

You leave us unaided forever
To starve and to thirst till the end
Surrendered to enemies clever
At strategy You comprehend.

48-end Remember the prayer I have longed for.
I've not left the others in vain.
The death I approach is a strong door;
To wrestle it open is pain.
I cannot escape from the battle
I've run from it too many times.
Prepare me before my last rattle.

Gethsemani strikes its last chimes,
It's time now to enter Your mercy
You promised to David the King.
His Son went this route; not in verse, He
Has trodden the truth, the real thing.

Look down on the shame of Your servants,
Our failures have made You the scorn
Of souls who are deep in disturbance
From Maine to Los Angeles, torn
Between the hostilities threatened
Within and without at Your Christ
And peace, which we're longing to get, and
The joy out of which we're enticed
Through Christ to the Father. The debt end,
Forgive it: His blood's sacrificed,
His body and blood are our Amen,
His Spirit has caught us like mice.

Thoughts Suggested by St Basil's Hymn:

Ἐπί σε χαίρει, κεχαριτωμένη

IN THEE REJOICES THE WHOLE WORLD

I—America

All water dances down
to the sea
in joy, because of thee
O Mary, full of grace
as the sea is full. Thy face
illumines the sun.
The birds of country and town
sing thy songs.
The lonely owl, for one,—
startled from its treetop at sundown—
screams of the Deposition,
while the cardinals' clear notes
coo of the tenderness of Bethlehem
and Nazareth. The ravens and the crows
call, call, call to the people
to rally to thy Son.
He has a banquet for the feeble
and from His side flows a ripple
of Blood, a drink for every one.
Pigeons and doves
once sacrificed for Him by thee
fly round triumphantly,
puff their chests in pride:
"Whoever flew, and lay dead too,
did you, for Jesus? We have died.

134

Joseph held us close as gloves
brought us to the very Temple.
Have you too? No, you've never seen
the glory where the High Priest's been
like we, the day of Simeon
and Anna." The seagulls seems to cry
around His tomb, like thy
myrrhbearing friends.
while the jay shouts, "He rose, He rose!"

Below the birds danced the trees.
Spruces, pines, and firs unfurled
thy banners to the world
in the prevailing breeze.
From the nor'east
for two days on end
beats the rain upon the melancholy beech
sheltering beast
and shadows, to lend
depth to woods and forest where the ravens preach.

The stable oak, fit for building homes,
is strong in deep contentment at the thought
of Nazareth, where Joseph's tools
were hung on her
and fashioned her with axe and hammer,
chisel, and saw, into use
even for thee and thy Son.
Perpetuate canticles of gnomes
who sit in branches, leaves, and sunbeams' stammer
playing their best but loose imitation of angels' fun:
the systematic song of all intelligence, to thee
O Garden, Woods thick with grace, and Field

where God was planted by His finger, strong
and powerfully fertile
for bringing life
perpetuating energies divine
even in us, which before
any light had shone or water fallen
blasted and blazed in thunderous volcanic glory—
The fingertip of uncreated energy is He,
the Spirit of thy Son, the shield
of vulnerable man and woman, long
tyrannized like turtle
exposed to knife
deprived of shield of shell against the fine
cutting thrust of evil, sore
from centuries of strife and unbelief and all on
beautiful wartorn praying planet Earth's sad story.

II—England

The lark in England's sky
sings joyfully that thou shalt never die
assumed to heaven, as thou wast
at Jesus' cost.
And quiet winter
waits for His return
and thine.
He will not stint a
summer beautiful, or burn
anything but chaff,
or kill the growing calf.
We hope to grow
like Peter's lambs,
and multiply, and sow

a harvest of little grams
of work and praise,
to sing our Mother's love
with our Creator, God above,
with all creation all our days,
long though we wandered other ways.

MY CANTICLE

A meditation on the Song of Songs. The numbers refer to the chapters in the biblical text.

I   Better than wine or whisky
      is a kiss from you
There's more life in your love
      than in cups of coffee
Your name is like poetry,
      two-syllable concert.
Call to me in your name
Drag me after you below the waves
Through the tunnels of the sea.
Past sharks and eels
And submarines of thirty-thousand tons
      eagerly I seek your pearls
Two eyes that saw
      before the sun detached its rays.

How right it is that I
      should let you love me
You only, oblivious
      of those I do not trust.
Though I'm repulsive
      to them, you chose me
And hung me on your wall

138

'Where you could stare at me,
　　take me and cosset me,
While the sun inside me burns
　　my mad mind learns
To reason peacefully.

Who has not been angry with me?
　　Disappointed, despising, disowning
For I let the weeds grow
　　then climbed the fence
　　to join your sheep
　　on someone else's hill.
I knew your voice
　　and loved it when I heard.
By my own choice
　　I came to where you pasture
among these rocks.
　　I rest with you, where
you feed your little flock.

I'm sorry for the sheep of other shepherds.
　　Let me not get too near;
I'll prance and ramp like a wild horse
　　if they come after.
You're my king, I'll wear your uniform
　　and not be kidnapped;
I'll wear the jewels you gave me
　　in my side and on my hands;
One love; your weapons:
　　my prayer, your word;
And ravish your pitying heart, for fear
　　you'll lose me.
Your golden word and silver sacrament.

Let me draw you, touch and see,
Let me know you rest in me
Till I smell of you
As though of burning leaves;
Until my eyes reflect your face
And know no other beauty can compare;
Until I bear a child to you,
And your house is ours.

II   Are you a flower for me to pick?
          or a wild one for me to find
     in the woods at the foot of two hills
          beside a running stream,
          an Indian spring,
     growing where no one I ever knew
          had seen you.
     Seen by me for the first and only time.
     How sweet is your flower
     Scenting the woods like lilies in a shower.

     Am I a single lily among briars
          surrounded by burrs
     Where neither sheep nor dogs may come,
          but only you with a brambling scythe
     Cutting carefully? Are you a tree,
          not for me to climb,
          but to sit under
     Picking your fruit from the ground?

          I found you, my lover,
     On a hot afternoon
          I rested in your shade
     I grew alone and chewed your apples.

The world became a banquet hall,
I sat alone with you
    and heard your silent word
Like a soft wind in the spring leaves
    stirring a soul.
I had no desire to walk farther
    as if I were not caressed
By your invisible arms.
    I'd rather wait
Until you make me love.

Some night you'll come and stop my breath
    like a deer appears from the trees
And stares into my delighted eyes;
    or like a thief who climbs the wall
And laughs at what he sees.
You'll call, I'll come, erect and eager,
    for the weather is good for a run
The ground soft to the feet,
    we'll run to the song of the new birds
Angelic in the sun.

III   Even on my bed I'll plan to find you,
    though you can't come there.
When I rise I'll go from place to place
    looking for you I love
Finding out from each person
    if he knows you
Or has seen you.
When I've asked them all,
    I'll find you.
All I'd wanted

in men and women,
Greek, Italian, liturgy and nature,
　　traveling through the world,
Prying into what is intimate
　　or superficial, I'll never want
To let go.
　　I'll hold you till it's time to wake.

You come across the sea
　　like a ferry
Smoking and pitching
　　casting the spray away.
Strong fishermen come with you,
　　their boats on either side,
　　expert in the sea,
　　to watch you capture me.
You have no fear,
　　confident as though it were a re-play.
You've built your ship of steel
　　riveted with iron
　　on a heavy keel.
　　Advancing like a lion
With hand on helm you pilot by the feel
　　you have for souls,
　　while the gulls squeal
and the souls gather at the wharf
　　you'll tie on.
This is the joy of your arrival.

IV　You think I'm beautiful
　　　　because I'm ugly;
　　　　my eyes are sad
　　　　from looking so long for you;

If I loved you as I should
    they'd cry behind the veil.
Why do I remind you of an animal
    gentle and clean, fertile and loving,
    and loveable? I do not know you.
Why treat me as though I were strong?
    Because your soldiers surround me?
Why do you love to lay your face on me,
    which I cannot see?
As if in some quiet woods we were alone,
    until the evening, when the shadows
    are in the treetops
And we are in the mountains
    high above the villages and towns.
There I burn the incense of my breath
    and pulse,
And you alone forget all the wrong
    I've done.
Raining blood, you wash it all away.
You write to me, leave the mountains, come.
    Descend from the haunts of lions.
Be tame, associate with women, boys, and men.
    For you'll protect me.
I do not need to snarl and run
    back to my mountain.
You recognize my clothes, you love my love,
    as if you were my brother
    or my bride, you keep me
As if I were a bottle of wine
    on your table,
A fragrant coffee-pot, steaming hot,
As if you liked to hear my talk,

under the holly tree, round the table,
Walled in, in privacy,
     where we laugh, our private glee
Is shared, we drink it like a spring.
     You sip my soul
I pour it out like nard upon you,
     the spice of life.
Rest at my well, at the foot of the hill
     catch your breath
     in the cool wind, the warm winds,
That blow the scent of blossoms past the walls.

V   You have come already
    You cannot find anything to eat or drink
        in all this anger
    So weed it out.
    But you have left. It is for me
        to weed your garden.
    I'll be beaten by the guards till it's done
        stripped to their lashes,
        contempt, and laughter.
    I'll moan out of longing for your return.

    People will tell me
        you're no better than any other,
    In fact you're over the hill,
        others are younger.
    But your complexion is spotless.
    This is the first day of your life.
    Your head is gold and needs no crown.
    Your hair never thin nor grey.
    Your eyes are quick, your teeth without cavity,

144

sharp to devour tough souls,
    hard and bright;
Yet children kiss your cheeks and lips,
    love to be lifted in your arms,
    and ride your great shoulders
Solid and secure on your own two feet,
    when you jump or sway,
That's why I want you for my friend.

VI   Will your saints help find you?
    You have come of your own accord
As the sun goes down, and not a bird is singing.
You have come to pick flowers,
    though it's winter.
Snow lies on piles of leaves.
    But you found what you wanted,
something more beautiful to you than Venice,
    more lovely than Palermo,
    gorgeous as Netherland flowers.
Your eyes are like the stars
    on long winter nights,
A fur coat is your hair, your smile
    is like a child's birthday
    for the awesome joy it spreads,
It tastes the cheek of your beloved.

No one was ever loved
so much as you, by so many;
No one by pity moved
so deep at less than a penny,
as though for an only child
whose mother had died in childbirth.—

Are many others now riled
To envy your gardening my wild earth?

For you are beautiful
In the early morning
Punctual, dutiful
Rising, like the yawning
Full moon at Easter-time,
Over Calvary splendid
To mark the feat, to chime
With clock-bells: the time of siege has ended.

I have come to the garden
        to pick vegetables you planted.
More than food, they are medicine
        for mortality, I could live on them
Forever, and grow better.
        People might look at me and not turn away.
The desire to die might leave me.

VII   On sandaled feet, in new-found health and strength,
        Drunk but sober, healthy but giving pleasure,
                Tall, eyes full of joyful water,
        Fearless before young men and wise,
                I could please you.
        You would reach for me,
                climb me like a tree,
                take hold of me
        Drink my energy to the last.
                I'll breathe my last low breath
                in your embraces.
        My failing strength belongs to you.
                (But why do you want it?)

146

Let us go into the fields,
 not running, and not to leave,
Stay into the long night
 for which there is no dawn.
It is time to press wine from the vine
 in the darkness;
It is time for one last dinner
 lasting forever.

VIII Death, you are my brother, I've come to visit.
 I will meet you out of doors
 I'll embrace you. You are the face of Christ.
You'll take me home, and reward me
 from your natural cellar.
Embrace me forever when it is time for love.
Our friends will see us
 coming together
Joined forever, where you woke me up
 as you woke my mother
And all our dead or murdered friends.

Tattoo me on your arm or chest,
 write my name in your breast,
Be my tombstone,
 let my memorial be hidden in you
Like a garden cleared in the forest
 under arching trees
Where a fire burns forever
 surrounded with stones
 and the scent of burning cedar.
A tidal wave or hurricane will not extinguish
 that happy flame
 dancing beyond all reason.

147

I could study all I wanted,
     buy an education,
It could not grant the wisdom
     of all-forgetting love
     where we lost the books from above
and never missed them.

Our courtship continues,
     on it you'll build the future.
Within its walls you've built your forts
     where I feel welcome,
     sheltered from every butcher.
The caretakers and guards protect
     its value, all for you.
The sea, the tide of fear, is checked,
     a single bird sings true
And calls to you, come quickly, come
To your flock, to all or some,
     or only one.

AUTOBIOGRAPHICAL NOTE

Elements in my rather introspective verse need to be explained by some autobiographical background, as the reader may wonder why there are references to such widely distant places as England, Maryland, the Narragansett Bay (Rhode Island), and Rome.

To start at the beginning: on November 20, 1926, the wife of the chaplain of Worcester College, Oxford, left a performance of *No, No, Nanette* at the New Theatre (accompanied by her sister-in-law, an American like herself), and gave birth to me at a nursing home on Walton Street opposite Worcester, in the row of houses which are now, I am told, a part of the college.

Over the next twenty-five years, important events in my life took place in that area between Worcester, Walton Street, and St Giles. My early childhood was spent around Worcester College, where my father was a fellow; but at Blackfriars on St Giles, in August of 1933, he and I were received into the Roman Catholic Church by the Dominican Father Bede Jarrett. In April 1952 I was ordained to the Catholic priesthood in the same Dominican church, while studying theology at Blackfriars as a member of St Benet's Hall. In between St Giles and Walton Street is 'The Studio,' a mews flat on Pusey Lane, where Jean and Sheldon Vanauken lived that year I was studying at Blackfriars, and my friendship with them and the circle of Christians who used to meet in 'The Studio' made a mark on my subsequent life.

Friendships do a lot towards forming one's personality, and mine with the Vanaukens encouraged my taste for Christianity and poetry, and for sharing them with people outside the pale of my own communion—not that I had not been involved in all those things already through my father, for whom religion, poetry, and friendships were the main things in life.

William Force Stead, my father, was an extremely gifted person. After leaving the University of Virginia, where he won his first prize for poetry, he went to England. There, after serving as U.S. Vice Consul in Nottingham and Liverpool, he studied for the ministry, and served as a Church of England curate in Ross-on-Wye and Florence, Italy. In between Ross and Florence, he took a degree in theology at Oxford, remaining a life-long friend of his tutor, Canon Streeter. In the twenties and thirties he achieved considerable fame for his poetry, some of which is included in the Oxford Book of Modern Verse and the Oxford Book of Christian Verse. Being the sort of man people love, he made an enormous number of friends, highly gifted people like himself. One, from his University of Virginia days, became a Supreme Court Justice, Stanley Reed. Some were theologians, like Canon Streeter, Bede Jarrett, and Martin D'Arcy. Others were poets and writers like himself: W.B. Yeats, T.S. Eliot (whom he baptized), Edmund Blunden, and—late in life—Tennessee Williams. The most fruitful period of his life, in my opinion, was the end, beginning in 1943, when he was Professor of English at Trinity College in Washington, D.C. Because he could communicate a *love* of his subject, he was a marvelous teacher. His only other child was a retarded boy, Philip, born in Liverpool, who died in Bristol in 1981 and is buried in Ross-on-Wye.

To return to my own life: the only place which has not triggered any poetry in me is the place where I spent my happiest years, Worth Priory (now an Abbey) in Sussex. I went to school there from the age of 8 to 12; it was an earthly paradise, for me. It is said that poetry and indeed all art is usually stimulated by pain or unhappiness of some kind; in my case, that has been true. Most of my verse is written prayer, stimulated by the natural hunger for God which is not a happy, though a normal, experience. I almost always felt that

150

hunger satisfied at Worth, both as a boy and on my return visits. Worth hardly inspired those bursts of anguished longing for something other than what was at hand, nor remorse, self-pity, or unrest.

During the summer vacation of 1939, my father took me on what was to be a month's visit to my grandfather and other relatives in the United States. Germany invaded Poland a week before we were to sail back, and my father and I, being on an American passport, were not permitted to return to England, now in the theater of war.

I then continued my schooling at Portsmouth Priory (now, like Worth, an Abbey) in Rhode Island, living during the vacations with the aunt in Maryland who had come to Oxford to help my parents at the time I was born. She, Mary Stead Worthington, became a second mother to me, and was the person by whom I have been loved more than by any other, hence important to my life, though I have never written a poem to her. (Perhaps our relationship was too happy?)

The main reason why Maryland is the subject of some of this verse is that I fell in love there for the first time. At about the same time, I felt an equally strong yearning for God in the monastic life. I made, I believe, the right choice in choosing God, but the pull of the opposite love produces a good deal of pain which has broken out from time to time in verse, sometimes feeling the human love as a symbol and call to the love of God. The choice has to be renewed daily, which makes of the monastic call a call to a certain degree of suffering. I do not regret making it; my only regret is that it has not been as wholehearted and joyous as it should have been.

After a year and three months working on farms in Maryland and Kentucky, I was accepted into the Benedictine monastery at Portsmouth. Most of this verse has come out of my life there, and at the college of Sant'Anselmo in Rome, where the monastery sent me to study. Some verse reflects my short stays at the monasteries of Fort Augustus in Scotland and Downside in the West of England.

151

Some of what was written when I was in Rome, or since, has been inspired by the spirituality of the "Focolare" Movement. I will not attempt here to capsulize the volumes which have been written to express this new development in Christian spirituality, initiated in 1943 (the year I entered the monastery) by Chiara Lubich in the North Italian city of Trent. The reader can drink it at its source in the many books published by Chiara or about her. It is sufficient to say that from the first moment I met her followers, the "Focolarini," I realized her spirituality was a gift, which could help me adjust the principles of monasticism to the twentieth century.

These autobiographical facts are necessary and sufficient to explain the emotional life expressed in this book of verse. I have not intended to put myself on display, but to share with my fellow creatures what may be either an echo or a stimulus of their own feelings for God, for man, and for God's created world of nature.

INDEX OF FIRST LINES

153